THE KEY TO EASTER

Vanessa Williams
Illustrated by Hannah Farmer

To order additional copies of this book, contact:
Xlibris
844-714-8691
www.Xlibris.com
Orders@Xlibris.com

ISBN: Softcover   978-1-6641-6269-3
       Hardcover   978-1-6641-6270-9
       EBook   978-1-6641-6268-6

Print information available on the last page

Rev. date: 03/18/2021

Once upon a time, there was a man and woman who lived in a wonderful, perfect world, a paradise. The animals could talk with them, and they had plenty of food to eat on all the trees. (I wonder if they had a cookie tree or maybe a chocolate tree!)

They had a wonderful Father who took care of them and loved them. He provided everything they would ever need or want. Their Father would tuck them in at night on a soft blanket of grass underneath the stars. The stars played music. They would listen to them as they fell asleep. Sometimes, the little lambs and lion cubs would cuddle up with them.

Everything was wonderful! They could go anywhere or do anything they wanted except eat from one of the trees in the middle of the garden. Their Father told them not to eat of that tree because they would die if they ate from it. The man and woman loved their Father, and their Father loved them. They never disobeyed him. They trusted him. They had plenty of things to do. They could play with the lions and wrestle with the monkeys. All the animals loved them and never ever tried to hurt them.

Then one day, a strange, funny animal came to the garden where the woman was alone. She was standing close to the tree the Father told them not to eat from. The animal was really funny and was laughing and talking with the woman. But he lied to her in order to trick her into eating from the tree. The animal said she would not die if she ate the fruit. The woman took a bite of the fruit, and nothing seemed to happen to her, but she felt really bad about what she had done.

When the man came over, she told him that it tasted pretty good, and he took a bite too. As soon as that happened, the strange, funny animal slithered to the side and started laughing. He had caused the man and woman to disobey the Father. A spiritual death happened to the man and woman. They were separated from the Father because of the seed of sin that was now sown in their hearts.

After a few minutes, a thick black fog gathered all around them and inside of them. Everything was hazy, and they could not see well through the black fog. The fog seemed to be getting thicker and darker as the day continued on. Death had entered into their world now. They felt so bad about what they had done. They both had disobeyed their Father.

It was like they were in a deep, dark, scary place now with that black fog all around them. They felt so sad in their heart, in their spirit. They felt dirty, ashamed, and embarrassed. The strange, funny animal just kept laughing and laughing at them with an evil laugh that sounded scary, and then it crept away. They ran and hid themselves behind bushes before their Father came to see them.

It wasn't long before their Father came to find them. They were so sad that they had disobeyed him. They were mad at themselves and at each other. They hid themselves and did not want to see him. (Always remember, that God will always forgive us. It is sometimes hard for us to forgive ourselves, but we must. We have to get out of the thick black fog.)

This hurt the Father so much. His heart was aching because he knew what would happen now. Their relationship would not be the same anymore. They would be separated from Him. The Father wanted to talk to the man and woman again so much. He wanted to laugh with them and talk with them and tuck them in at night underneath the stars.

Their Father came every day trying to talk to them or get a glimpse of them. He longed for their company so much. But now they were separated from Him, and they missed their Father very much. This went on for a long, long time, and the black fog kept getting thicker and thicker between them until, one day, the man and woman could not even see or hear their Father anymore.

The man and woman soon had children of their own. They told their children about their Father. Their children had never seen the Father, and they really did not know if He existed at all. Years went by, and more and more children were born. They started thinking maybe it was just a made-up story, make-believe, not really true at all. The Father was so heartbroken. Hardly anyone knew about Him anymore, and nobody tried to talk to Him. There was nobody that could get through to the people in the thick black fog of sin.

The Father really wanted to get to know the people again. He wanted to love them and care for them the same way He had the man and woman. He decided that He would have to make a way where there seemed to be no way. The Father came up with a big plan to get the people in the thick black fog to hear Him and see Him again. The fog was so thick and so black and so deep.

The people needed a KEY to get out of that thick black fog and into the Father's House in the Father's Kingdom. They had some keys there in the fog. Some people had success keys, some had education keys. They studied and became really smart about the things in the thick black fog. Some had power and wealth keys in the thick black fog. Some had a key to a really awesome car that they could drive around in the black fog. Some had keys to huge houses in the thick black fog. Some had hotel keys to far-away corners of the thick black fog. But nobody, not one, had a key to the Father's Kingdom. They had heard about His Kingdom from their grandmothers and grandfathers, but they really didn't know for sure that such a place existed.

The only way a person could ever get into the thick black fog world was to be born there as a baby. So that was what the Father made happen. It was a miracle. One day, some Holy Ghost Power, some awesome "talking in tongues, walking on water, raising the dead" power happened to a young girl who lived right in the middle of the deep, dark, thick black fog. A few months later, she gave birth to the Father's baby boy. She named him JESUS! The young girl was His mother, and He was the Son of the Father. This miracle happened in the thick black fog.

Jesus, the Son of the Father, grew up and talked to all the people in the black fog, even the little boys and girls. He taught them about His Kingdom. He told them how their world was in the beginning with the very first man and woman. He told them how it was before they disobeyed and the thick black fog separated them from their Father. He told them about the animals being friendly, the soft green grass, and the stars that sing you to sleep at night. He told them how it was full of righteousness, peace, and joy. Some people believed Him and asked Him how to get into His Kingdom. They were so excited.

Other people, however, were angry with Him. Their hearts were so full of the thick black fog, and they had accumulated a lot of keys in the thick black fog. They did not want to leave it for His Kingdom. They could not see Him for who He was: the Son of the Father. They could not even understand what He was saying. Some were so angry with Him that they killed Him. They put nails in His hands and feet and hung Him on a cross. They made fun of Him until He died there in that thick black fog.

That strange, funny animal had come back and tricked the people into killing the Father's Son. He did not realize that the Father was the one who was tricking him this time! After they killed the Father's Son, they put His body in a tomb, which was an even thicker, blacker place in the thick black fog, and left Him there. Little did they know, that was just what the Father wanted them to do.

The Son had to die there in that thick black fog in order to conquer death, hell, and the grave. The Father knew that once His Son died, He would resurrect and come back to life again. That death and resurrection would provide the KEY for all the people to get out of the thick black fog and into the Father's kingdom and into his presence once again.

The thick black fog came when the first man disobeyed. He ate from the tree that his Father told him not to eat from. The Father's Son, JESUS, was without sin; He never disobeyed, and that was the only way to get out of the thick black fog. JESUS was a son that never disobeyed the Father, and He never did anything wrong. JESUS did not have any of the thick black fog in Him or in His heart. The Father was able to reach Him from the deepest, darkest part of the thick black fog and bring Him back to life.

JESUS was alive again. He walked around to show everyone that He was alive and that He had made a way where there seemed to be no way. He was the KEY! Nobody could get to the Father and His Kingdom except through Him. Jesus is the WAY, the TRUTH, and the LIFE. His death, burial, and resurrection made a way for all of us to be able to do the same thing now. We can be born again out of the thick black fog of sin and come into the Father's Kingdom.

Has anyone ever told you that God loves you and that He has a wonderful plan for your life? If you were to die this very second, do you know for sure, that you would go to Heaven

Let me quickly share with you what the Holy Bible reads. It reads "for all have sinned and come short of the glory of God" and "for the wages of sin is death, but the gift of God is eternal life through Jesus Christ our Lord". The Bible also reads, "For whosoever shall call upon the name of the Lord shall be saved".

I'm going to say a quick prayer for you. Lord, bless the person reading this book and their family with long and healthy lives. Jesus, make Yourself real to them and do a quick work in their heart. If they have not received Jesus Christ as Lord and Savior, I pray they will do so now.

Just say the following and really mean it in your heart: Dear Lord Jesus, come into my heart. Forgive me of my sin. Wash me and cleanse me. Set me free. Jesus, thank You that You died for me. I believe that You are risen from the dead and that You're coming back again for me. Fill me with the Holy Spirit. Give me a passion for the lost, a hunger for the things of God and a holy boldness to preach the gospel of Jesus Christ. I'm saved; I'm born again, I'm forgiven and I'm on my way to Heaven because I have Jesus in my heart.

Amen.

Printed in the United States
by Baker & Taylor Publisher Services